**ENEMY OF THE STATE**

**DISPARATE TREATMENT**

IT'S DANGEROUS TO BE RIGHT WHEN
THE GOVERNMENT IS WRONG!

By: James Coe Jr., B.S.E.E.

# Enemy Of The State

Disparate Treatment

James Coe Jr., B.S.E.E.

# Enemy Of The State

Disparate Treatment

James Coe Jr., B.S.E.E.

This book is dedicated in the loving memory of my life long best friend Robert Tyrone Bell.

Sunrise for him was January 16, 1948 and sunset for him was February 27, 1990 in my arms at the Veteran's Administration Medical Center in Philadelphia, Pennsylvania.

Before he passed on, he said "never take your boots off, for you the war will never end".

# Enemy Of The State

Disparate Treatment

James Coe Jr., B.S.E.E.

# Enemy Of The State

Disparate Treatment

James Coe Jr., B.S.E.E.

# Table of Contents

Chapter 1: The Racism Matrix .................................................... 8
    THE NATURE OF RACISM IN THE GOVERNMENT ........ 8
    PROTECTING MY INDEPENDENCE ................................. 8
    THE THREE LEVELS OF THE MASSIVE GOVERNMENT PYRAMID ................................................................................ 9
    THE NUMBERS GAME: WHO BELIEVES THE GOVERNMENT RHETORIC? ................................................. 9
    BACKGROUND ......................................................................... 10
    THE RACE CARD .................................................................... 11
    THE PURGE .............................................................................. 12
    THE TRUTH .............................................................................. 13
    911 CALLS: THREATS MADE INSIDE A GOVERNMENT BUILDING .................................................................................. 14
Chapter 2: The Context Matrix .................................................... 16
    MY STORY ................................................................................ 16
    FROM LIFE TO DEATH ........................................................... 17
    INDEPENDENCE IS YOUR RIGHT ...................................... 18
Chapter 3: The Terrorism Matrix .................................................. 20
    TERRORISM IN THE WORKPLACE .................................... 20
    THE TERRORISM MATRIX .................................................. 20
    VIRUS ECONOMICS .............................................................. 21
    THE GOVERNMENT LABELS MATRIX ............................. 22
Chapter 4: The Collusion and Conspiracy Matrix ..................... 24
    THE COLLUSION AND CONSPIRACY BLUEPRINT ....... 24
    THE LABOR DISPUTE ADMINISTRATIVE PROCESS MATRIX REVEALED ............................................................... 24
    THE SMOKING GUNS ........................................................... 26
    Some Legal Questions ............................................................. 27
    THE DIRTY LITTLE SECRET ............................................... 27
    THE CRITICAL DATE MATRIX .......................................... 28

# Enemy Of The State

Disparate Treatment

James Coe Jr., B.S.E.E.

```
STATE OF NEW JERSEY AFFIRMS MY POSITION .......29
LAST CHANCE AGREEMENT SETTLEMENT .................30
THE ARBITRATION AWARD.............................................32
THE AWARD SUMMARY ...................................................33
THE DISPUTE ISSUE:..........................................................33
THE U.S. JUSTICE DEPARTMENT.....................................36
```

# Enemy Of The State

Disparate Treatment

James Coe Jr., B.S.E.E.

Chapter 5: The Workplace Matrix .................................................38
   I'M UNDER GOVERNMENT ATTACK ..............................38
Chapter 6: The DNA Fingerprints Matrix.................................44
   HISTORY VS. RACE...........................................................46
   CONSIDER THE MATH HERE TO PROVE A
   MISCONDUCT CONSPIRACY: ...........................................49
Chapter 7: The Smoking Guns Matrix.........................................53
   THE NSA TERROR WATCH LIST .......................................55
   THERE ARE NO RIGHTS IF YOU CANNOT DEFEND
   THEM...................................................................................56
   YOU MUST KNOW YOUR LEGAL OPTIONS ...................56
   THE THREE ADMINISTRATIVE APPEALS PROCESSES
   DOCUMENTS .......................................................................58

# Enemy Of The State

Disparate Treatment

James Coe Jr., B.S.E.E.

# Enemy Of The State

Disparate Treatment

James Coe Jr., B.S.E.E.

## Chapter 1: The Racism Matrix

**THE NATURE OF RACISM IN THE GOVERNMENT**

My name is James Coe, and I am fighting for my life. I might as well have been deemed an enemy of the state. Welcome to my world.

The government stopped my income. Paralyzed with fear, shame, and hopelessness, I withdrew from *everyone* and everything around me. I had lost all my self-respect. I was afraid to open my mail. I was afraid to answer the telephone. Paralyzed by my fear and self-doubt, I could either choose to let it guide me or drag me down.

When the government attacks, the problem is it is hard to recognize that one is being attacked. In fact, it is when turning to the government for help that one's problems only seem to increase.

I have come to the conclusion that the government is unethical. Independence is the enemy of fear and self-doubt, thus I must fight back.

**PROTECTING MY INDEPENDENCE**

# Enemy Of The State

Disparate Treatment

James Coe Jr., B.S.E.E.

If I want to protect my independence, it is imperative that I believe that I, not the government, am steering the wheel of my own independence, especially my economic independence. In fact, I have developed a mathematical economic formula which I intend to reveal at some point.

Firstly, I am a former federal union employee. Secondly, I was wrongfully accused of misconduct on the job. Thirdly, I was removed without Collective Bargaining Agreement rights. I respectfully intend to make an argument for disparate treatment based on race to support my argument to reveal gross misconduct at the highest levels of the government pyramid.

## THE THREE LEVELS OF THE MASSIVE GOVERNMENT PYRAMID

Before I continue, I feel it is necessary to give you a brief refresher course on government infrastructure. There are three levels of the government. Each level has its elected representatives.

The three levels of the government pyramid are as follows:

The first government level can be called the local government. Examples of the local government include cities, townships, counties, and boroughs. The second level includes state government agencies. The third level is the federal government, which is sometimes casually referred to as "the feds".

# Enemy Of The State

Disparate Treatment

James Coe Jr., B.S.E.E.

## THE NUMBERS GAME: WHO BELIEVES THE GOVERNMENT RHETORIC?

While doing field research for this document, I decided to go to the people.
I took a little survey, and I asked 25 people one question: "What percentage of government information do you believe?"

The average response I got in my informal survey ranged from between 10%-30% of participants "believing" government information. What was surprising was that no citizen stated a number above 50%.

## BACKGROUND

I am a Dysfunctional Vietnam Era Disabled Veteran. I served in the U.S. Army from 1965-68. I earned a Bachelor's of Science in Electrical Engineering (B.S.E.E.) from Temple University College of Engineering. In addition, I earned ten Computer, Internet, and Networking Technology Certifications. I completed post grad courses in advanced software operating system design at MIT. I completed post grad courses in advanced business strategy at the Harvard School of Business. My knowledge is current on any internet technology.

I worked for the Postal Service as a GS-4 Mail-handler for

# Enemy Of The State

Disparate Treatment

James Coe Jr., B.S.E.E.

---

seventeen years without a single promotion; in other words, *"niggers"* need not apply. I was denied advancement twenty-one times by my manager Tony Brullo and the management staff.

I served three years as an Army Postal Officer MOS 71F20, after completing the Army's six months Postal Operations School at Ft. Benjamin Harrison, Indiana. My Army level converts directly to a level GS-25 Postmaster civilian equivalent.

## RACE CARD

The dirty little secret of my story focuses on the issue of racism in the workplace as the hidden motivation for disparate treatment by high level government officials with the power and the authority to manipulate the outcome of the administrative process. For the record, under our system of justice, if the defendant is the U.S. government, there must be zero tolerance for administrative process errors. If at anytime there is any reasonable doubt introduced, then I have proven my argument for racism being the hidden motivation behind the adverse employment actions taken against me in the court of public opinion, because during the administrative process in most states, like the state of New Jersey, you're denied a hearing by jury. In most states an administrative judge will make

# Enemy Of The State

Disparate Treatment

James Coe Jr., B.S.E.E.

the final decision in a labor dispute.

The Contact Profile Demographics Traits:

| Name | Race | Sex | Position | PPP Impact |
|---|---|---|---|---|
| Cannavo | White | M | Arbitrator | Issued Opinion |
| Pacheco | White | M | SPM | Decision Maker |
| Szpyhulsky | White | M | MDO | Decision Maker |
| Brullo | White | M | SDO | Supervisor |
| DuPree | Black | F | Investigator | Decision Maker |
| Kastner | White | M | Lawyer | Legal Advisor |
| NJ Labor Depart | Hispanic | F | Investigator | Issued Opinion |
| MSPB | Black | F | Judge | Issued Opinion |

I put together a profile of the contacts based on several factors, and then I discovered a unique pattern based on race with regard to the opinions and the decision makers with regards to the PPP (Prohibited Personnel Policy) facts in my case. All the females consistently disagree with the white males with regard to the facts in this labor dispute, and their opinions all are consistently in favor of no misconduct on my part. On the other hand, all the white males take the opposite side of the fence.

For the purpose of my argument I define white racism as an act of discrimination against a minority, in particular, by one who is privileged or in a position of power over the minority. In relation to the workplace, racism is rogue discrimination or misconduct by government officials in a position of power, authority, or direct economic leverage.

White Racism is also demonstrated through applying a mindset strategy based on race, in the workplace, to a prohibited personnel policy, also referred to as a PPP, in

# Enemy Of The State

Disparate Treatment

James Coe Jr., B.S.E.E.

order to direct or manipulate the PPP outcome.

## THE PURGE

In today's workplace, race still matters. For the context of my argument, I must reveal that I am a black male employee of the Postal Service at, Kilmer Mail Processing & Distribution Center, Edison, New Jersey, and that my boss (Tony Brullo) is a white male. At 18:00 hours on April 1, 2005, I was over fifty years old. I mention my age because age discrimination travels deep below the surface and is often over looked as a potential "type" of discrimination in my argument.

My work assignment on this day, April 1, 2005, was the "LCTS" (Low-Cost Tray-Sorter), which when operational, generally requires ten to twenty employees to operate the machine. On April 1, 2005 I was the top senior union employee out of twenty union employees assigned to First Class Mail Breakdown.

The day had started just like any other normal work day until lunchtime when Brullo ordered everyone to lunch except a mail clerk, Sharon Ruszczyk, and me. I felt very odd when SDO Brullo ordered the whole section to lunch at 20:00 hours, leaving me alone. It was odd--the most senior employee totally isolated from all the other co-workers. From that point forward, my lifestyle would be changed forever because of my race.

# Enemy Of The State

Disparate Treatment

James Coe Jr., B.S.E.E.

## THE TRUTH

SDO Brullo had harassed me several times by following me every time he saw me go into the men's room. At some point, it made me very uncomfortable. I wanted to wish it away, but I could not. I was forced to file an in-house EEOC Harassment Complaint against SDO Brullo to correct his offensive behavior. Upon exiting the men's room on April 1, 2005, I asked SDO Brullo several times why he followed me into the men's room.

As a white manager, SDO Brullo holds a bias, using his position of power and authority to manipulate a prohibited personnel practice (Insubordination) which would result in economic harm to the employee: being fired.

There are three sides to this story: the hype, the truth, and the results. Both the hype and the truth are revealed inside the "Step 1: Grievance Summary" (DNA#3). The results are revealed inside the Arbitration Award (DNA#7).

After I exited the men's room on April 1, 2005, SDO Brullo stated that he was going to fire me. I asked him for what reason, to which he responded that I must go with him into his office, and that he would think of something.

Next, I was instantly placed on "Emergency-Placement-In-Off-Duty-Status" charged with "Insubordination" (DNA#2), which was in direct violation of the disciplinary procedure set forth in Article 16.7 of the National Union Agreement. In order to be placed in the above employee status, you must be in a state of intoxication or charged with drug or alcohol use, pilferage, or failure to observe safety rules or

# Enemy Of The State

Disparate Treatment

James Coe Jr., B.S.E.E.

---

regulations. I was never charged with intoxication (use of drugs or alcohol), pilferage, or failure to observe safety rules or regulations.

## 911 CALLS: THREATS MADE INSIDE A GOVERNMENT BUILDING

Before placing me in Emergency Placement In Off-Duty Status, out of fear for his own safety, SDO Brullo made a 911 call to the Edison Police claiming I was making threats in a postal facility. Any post September 11, 2001 (9/11) 911 call using the word "threats" inside a government Postal facility will trigger a massive law enforcement reaction. Once the police dispatcher enters the 911 government terror threat code, it can never be recalled or erased from the database. In addition, in a post 9/11 world, this code triggers an instant NSA investigation to close out the call.

First, I need to put events into context based on a timeline to show that my educational and military history were outstanding. I worked in a very hostile Postal Service workplace for seventeen years where unchecked racial harassment was more the norm. I find it to be racist that my EEOC rights, Union rights, and MSPB Vietnam Era Veterans Rights were all blatantly violated without just cause or due process. I was also blacklisted by top level Postal Service decision makers. I was denied advancement at every opportunity, which resulted in me getting twenty-one "Good Luck Next Time" letters spanning seventeen years.
Brullo and the management staff failed to complete the

# Enemy Of The State

Disparate Treatment

James Coe Jr., B.S.E.E.

employee review section, which automatically disqualified my application for promotion. There was no way to reverse or overcome management Disparate Treatment.

# Enemy Of The State

Disparate Treatment

James Coe Jr., B.S.E.E.

## Chapter 2: The Context Matrix

**MY STORY**

My journey starts with child abuse. I suffered greatly from child abuse growing up, until I was forced to join the U.S. Army. The Army was not what I would call a safe house for abused children -- far from it.

I attended Thomas A. Edison High School. Edison was an all-black boy's inner city school in one of the highest crime districts in North Philadelphia. To put things into focus, sixty to seventy young black men were dying in gang wars annually in the city nicknamed "the city of brotherly love". In the 60s, black eighteen year old men were half American citizens. Blacks had no political power, nor did they vote. During the Vietnam War Era, blacks were drafted and forced to die for America!

I remember just like it was yesterday, about two months after high school ended. Every kid that had finished high school got a draft notice in the mail. The city draft board went down the high school graduation list name by name.

I recall that after finishing basic training, you got to spend two weeks with your family and friends before you went straight to Vietnam. We were just young kids drafted to serve and die for the government.

# Enemy Of The State

Disparate Treatment

James Coe Jr., B.S.E.E.

## FROM LIFE TO DEATH

I became a part of Vietnam American History after my high school class of 1965 Thomas Edison High, Philadelphia Pennsylvania, suffered the highest Vietnam Era casualty rate in American history of eighty percent!

My class of 1965 was given the Presidential Service Medal by President L.B. Johnson. The President spent one tension filled day with the black community mothers of my fallen classmates. The tension that day was so thick that you could have cut it with a knife!

I was blessed to survive and later battled my way to a four year Electrical Engineering degree from Temple University with the help of the Vietnam Era G.I. Bill.

However, after several near death experiences in my life, I began to wonder "*why me*".

On Tuesday, February 27, 1990, my best and only friend, Robert Tyrone Bell, died in my arms at the Philadelphia Veteran's Administration Medical Center. Robert died of "Agent Orange", which causes cancer. I spent the final hours with him, in which we relived the good old days. Before Robert passed, he suddenly warned me about my life in the future. He shocked the hell of me, to be perfectly honest.

# Enemy Of The State

Disparate Treatment

James Coe Jr., B.S.E.E.

---

I'll never forget his final words: "Brother, never take your boots off. For you, the war will never end".

After that day, I would have visions about the future, but I paid my visions little mind until I would see events that were going to harm me in the future.

Most recently, I saw the World Trade Center attack, because I once worked in the WTC on the 72nd floor in tower II, which was where the second plane hit.
In addition, I also predicted two future city mayors, years in advance of their elections. The first mayor elect prediction was then Philadelphia, Pennsylvania Assistant District Attorney, also my Temple University Criminal Justice professor and later Pennsylvania Governor elect, Ed Rendell. The second mayor elect prediction was then Piscataway, New Jersey Councilman Brian Wahler.

## INDEPENDENCE IS YOUR RIGHT

I'm maybe a little old fashioned, but I truly believe every citizen should try to live his or her life on his or her own terms. I believe you can live your dreams, if you're willing to fight for them. Don't ever allow the government to steal your dreams. Fight back!

# Enemy Of The State

Disparate Treatment

James Coe Jr., B.S.E.E.

# Enemy Of The State

Disparate Treatment

James Coe Jr., B.S.E.E.

## Chapter 3: The Terrorism Matrix

### TERRORISM IN THE WORKPLACE

I have noticed that a lot of struggling veterans have really lost their will to fight back. We talk a lot about freedom that Americans have, and many times, if you're a victim of disparate treatment and oppression, you can't really partake of the freedoms we have earned. I want to fight back for the veterans and people who don't have a voice, and to maybe even empower them to advocate for themselves.

I need to reveal a little known secret fact here.

This secret will also explain the title of this book *Enemy Of The State Fights Back: It's Dangerous To Be Right When The Government Is Wrong!*

I have a belief that terrorism is a "virus" that can be studied.

I have trademarked the phrase "Terrorism Matrix" and developed a mathematical formula.

### THE TERRORISM MATRIX

TERRORISM MATRIX = ECONOMICS (divided by)

# Enemy Of The State

Disparate Treatment

James Coe Jr., B.S.E.E.

POWER

I'm going to use a metaphor to explain and show that terrorism in the workplace is a virus, not just a media news event. What is known about viruses is that they change or mutate over time. Also, note that terrorism in the workplace is a form or mutation of *"workplace racism"*, which I introduced in chapter one. The difference or mutational element that is added to workplace racism is the economic mutation component. Most viruses tend to stay ahead of the curve in terms of detection, in my case. I'm speaking directly about the labor dispute administrative process outcome.

The purpose of the labor dispute administrative process is to review all the facts and issues with an *"unbiased decision."* To properly stop workplace racism, we must address its dirty little roots: *"government misconduct"*, i.e. disparate treatment in the workplace.

**VIRUS ECONOMICS**

Now try to imagine working forty-seven years in America, and at sixty-six, which is retirement age for the average person, you get $0.00 Social Security income.
The other half of my work history was seventeen years of federal employment. I'm still not getting my federal employment pension income.

Now imagine you're like many Afro-Americans today that

# Enemy Of The State

Disparate Treatment

James Coe Jr., B.S.E.E.

---

will have higher healthcare costs because of their ethnic group. As a group, we tend to suffer more from high blood pressure and prostate cancer.

How, as an Afro-American, can I manage the healthcare cost associated with high blood pressure (silent killer; no warnings given) or prostate cancer treatment without income? Now I have a double death sentence. In addition, how will I survive on the streets if I'm homeless after I lose my home to foreclosure or a tax sale?

**THE GOVERNMENT LABELS MATRIX**

Beware: these labels can also be used as weapons to cause you harm

* Insubordination
* Bi-polar Disorder
* Mental Depression Disorder
* Bankruptcy
* Terrorist | Threats
* Criminal Arrests
* ADHD
* Age Discrimination
* Whistleblower

Labels are big brother's tools of the trade.

Coming next: my "Big Brother's Toolbox | Weapons Matrix."

# Enemy Of The State

Disparate Treatment

James Coe Jr., B.S.E.E.

The next question is: how do I protect myself against big brother label abuse? The short answer is: know your civil rights.

# Enemy Of The State

Disparate Treatment

James Coe Jr., B.S.E.E.

# Enemy Of The State

Disparate Treatment

James Coe Jr., B.S.E.E.

## Chapter 4: The Collusion and Conspiracy Matrix

### THE COLLUSION AND CONSPIRACY BLUEPRINT

* FORENSIC REVERSE-ENGINEERING PROCESS

Part I: Collective Bargaining Agreement - Article 16: Discipline Procedure

Part II: Collective Bargaining Agreement - Article 15: Grievance Procedure

Part III: Review and Integrate Parts I & Part II to confirm or reverse the agency final decision.

Conduct a forensic review of the grievance and the discipline procedures based on the forensic documents from the government's labor dispute on April 1, 2005.

### THE LABOR DISPUTE ADMINISTRATIVE PROCESS MATRIX REVEALED

### Independence = Power/Economics

* Last Chance Settlement Agreement - December 8, 2004 (DNA#6)

# Enemy Of The State

Disparate Treatment

James Coe Jr., B.S.E.E.

* Emergency Placement In Off-Duty Status - April 1, 2005 (DNA#2)

* Step 1: Grievance Summary - April 21, 2005 (DNA#3)

* Step 2: Grievance Designee - May 12, 2005 (DNA#10)

* Notice of Proposed Removal - May 5, 2005 (DNA#8)

* Letter of Decision - June 15, 2005 (DNA#9)

* New Jersey Labor Appeal Tribunal - July 31, 2005 (DNA#4)

* Arbitration Award - October 10, 2007 (DNA#7)

I am going to reverse - engineer my conspiracy argument starting with a timeline overview.

The newsworthy story is that, under the law, my Vietnam Era Veteran's employment rights were grossly violated by the government because I did not get, nor did I have, all the critical government documents listed here in order to point out gross government misconduct during the administrative process.

The government's only position has been the untimely defense, not the massive government misconduct during the administrative process.

For example: the fact that I waived my right to testify at a

# Enemy Of The State

Disparate Treatment

James Coe Jr., B.S.E.E.

manipulated Arbitration Hearing on October 10, 2007 (DNA#7) reveals the agency's disparate treatment tactic to deny my Collective Bargaining Agreement rights and fire me without just cause. Also, I was offered $2,000 by the Postal Service to walk away during the administrative process.

If the U.S. Justice Department investigates and reviews all the documents, specifically the Step 2: Grievance Letter from Designee (DNA#10) Gwendolyn DuPree on May 12, 2005 to Tom Hynes, my Union representative, the Emergency Placement In Off-Duty Status grievance was withdrawn along with any related grievances.

However, the Notice of Proposed Removal issued by SDO Brullo and his boss MDO John Szpyhulsky on May 5, 2005 was in clear conflict with DuPree's letter dated May 12, 2005. The final outcome makes the May 12, 2005 letter from Step 2: designee Gwendolyn DuPree misleading at best, or false.

What's even more misleading are the dates listed on the Notice of Proposed Removal. The dates clearly exhibit a conspiracy that DuPree may or may not be a party to given the fact that DuPree is a black female. I am going to err on the side of not being a party!

The U.S. Justice Department needs to investigate the extremely inconsistent labor relations case history.

Also note that, all the dates listed on the agency's Notice of Proposed Removal, signed by SDO Brullo and MDO John Szphyhulsky were all pre-dated before the May 12, 2005

# Enemy Of The State

Disparate Treatment

James Coe Jr., B.S.E.E.

---

Step 2: Grievance Letter issued by DuPree.

## THE SMOKING GUNS

In DuPree's letter, she clearly states all grievances related to Coe will be withdrawn.

The trick is there were no grievances filed on any of these dates listed on the Notice of Proposed Removal; therefore, the Union never grieved, which means there was no discipline issued. I was never disciplined on any of those dates by any of the hearsay managers listed on the record (DNA#8 and DNA#9).

This is another clear example of institutional racism.

At best, this should trigger a full U.S. Justice Department investigation into my Civil Rights violations and a NAACP letter of protest.

## Some Legal Questions

Does this sound like a conspiracy?

Does this confirm race based discrimination, given SDO Brullo's history?

Does anything here smell like collusion during the grievance process?

# Enemy Of The State

Disparate Treatment

James Coe Jr., B.S.E.E.

It's all about the Matrix applying a mindset based on racism, which is defined as power divided by economic income.

There is no way to know any of the legal after math of DuPree's Step 2: Grievance Letter to Union representative Tom Hynes until after the Notice of Removal by Plant Manager Pacheco. I was clearly confused by Pacheco's June 15, 2005 "Letter of Decision" (DNA#9), which referenced hearsay statements which made no sense.

## THE DIRTY LITTLE SECRET

The dirty little secret that, I said I would reveal on the inside is the fact that Senior Plant Manager Victor Pacheco signed both the Merit System Protection Board, Last Chance Settlement Agreement (DNA#6), and not to err on the side of fairness, he later issued the agency's Final Decision Letter, which officially ended my employment (DNA#9). Pacheco's actions demonstrate both a conflict of interest and disparate treatment.

What happened to the next level review for fairness? What appears to be consistent in my life is the disparate treatment by management across the board. I was not fired on any of the days listed in the Letter of Decision, nor was I disciplined on any of those days.

# Enemy Of The State

Disparate Treatment

James Coe Jr., B.S.E.E.

## THE CRITICAL DATE MATRIX

The only date that is legally critical is April 1, 2005. Let me explain why I say that it's ground zero in my argument. Simply put: this is the trigger date. This is the date the adverse prohibited personnel practice was taken against me. This is the date the charges were given to me in writing by SDO Brullo. This is the date I reported to unemployment in the box which asks, *"What date were you fired?"* This is the date the unemployment office used to calculate my unemployment benefits starting date. If you are found to be fired for cause, i.e. insubordination, you will be denied unemployment benefits. If you choose to appeal, which is your right, you are about to enter into the tricky world I call the *"Administrative Appeals Process"*. In short, this is where your real rights are denied or granted. This is where all the other dates fit into the matrix.

For example, the December 8, 2004 date mentioned throughout this document is the date of my administrative judge hearing before the Merit System Protection Board. All veterans have this extra level of protection during the administrative appeals process. The smoking gun on that date was two-fold:

(1)     Per the National Agreement, the Union failed to witness the document.
(2)     The document violated the National Agreement by changing my conditions of employment, i.e. disparage of treatment, without written union approval.

Finally, this brings into question: why did I sign the LCA, and the simple answer is that I paid to have legal

# Enemy Of The State

Disparate Treatment

James Coe Jr., B.S.E.E.

---

representation. I questioned the content of the document several times. After several LCA document revisions and several heated exchanges between me and my lawyer, Mr. Kastner, the tone of the document changed very little from the beginning.

I signed the LCA document because I felt I had no other choice. I just wanted to get the hell out of there. I wanted to focus on April 1, 2005 and what actually happened on that date, because if the facts are not true, then there was no prohibited personnel policy as initially reported by SDO Brullo to the New Jersey Department of Labor. I must turn this administrative process into a criminal misconduct process. For the record, if there was any knowledge of "fraud", i.e. willfully filing false labor reports to another government agency, it is the fact that SDO Brullo failed to state a Prima Facie case before the Merit System Protection Board by refusing under oath to state why he discharged me. In a perfect world, the rights of all veterans are protected regardless of race. By the way, this is not a perfect world.

## STATE OF NEW JERSEY AFFIRMS MY POSITION

The New Jersey Appeals Tribunal Docket No.: 85, 028 investigated the facts (DNA#4) in this labor dispute and issued a decision that there was no misconduct related to job performance as alleged by the U.S. Postal Service against me. In fact, the New Jersey Labor Department issued a fine against the U.S. Postal Service for filing a false labor report. The Appeal Tribunal strongly recommended that I, the employee, be returned to duty with full benefits.

# Enemy Of The State

Disparate Treatment

James Coe Jr., B.S.E.E.

## LAST CHANCE AGREEMENT SETTLEMENT

The LCA players include: the Agency (conspiracy) Lawyer Rowe, the (collusion) Plant Manager Pacheco, and my (ineffective) lawyer, Mitchell Kastner, Esq.

The fact is the Union's Thomas Hynes, present at the Merit System Protection Board Hearing on December 8, 2004, failed to sign the Last Chance Settlement, which makes the Settlement Agreement highly illegal and therefore not enforceable under the Collective Bargaining Agreement, i.e. Arbitration (DNA#7).

Another smoking gun that makes the Settlement Agreement highly illegal is the fact it unlawfully changes the Terms and Conditions of my Employee Working Conditions without written Union approval. In other words, the Last Chance Settlement did in fact show disparate treatment against me based on race.

I think the U.S. Justice Department would use the legal term "government misconduct" or "fraud" to make a case to reverse this decision.

For the record, I need to explain the condition I was under when I signed the LCA on December 8, 2004. I have had nightmares and trouble sleeping ever since that day.

The hearing before MSPB Judge Sandra Squire started at

# Enemy Of The State

Disparate Treatment

James Coe Jr., B.S.E.E.

---

9:30am. Postal Service's SDO Brullo was the first to testify before the court. For the record, Brullo was asked repeatedly by Judge Squire to tell the court what happened and why there should be a hearing before the court on the facts. In legal terms this is called making a prime facie case. In other words, the agency must state on the record a set of facts under oath that violate a prohibited personnel policy under the Collective Bargaining Agreement. Brullo attempted several times to respond with hearsay testimony about what other people told him, and every time the judge disallowed Brullo's testimony as hearsay. The judge ordered Brullo to testify only about his personal experience before the court. Brullo then failed to give any direct testimony, and he refused to speak. The judge asked him five times: "is that your last response?" she waited about five minutes and then she said the hearing was closed.

The hearing before Judge Squire ended at 9:45 a.m. when she ordered the parties to draft a settlement agreement.

What happened next shocked and surprised me and frankly ended my employment without due process. Let me put things into context. After the judge ended the hearing, I went to the restroom, and then I waited in the Judge's chamber room while my attorney and the agency attorney made a call to David Friedman, the agency legal team director. They were on the telephone for over an hour discussing the critical details of my settlement agreement without me or my union representative, Thomas Hynes who was present with me.

By law, after the Postal Service failed to make a case inside the courtroom, the attorneys should have stepped aside,

# Enemy Of The State

Disparate Treatment

James Coe Jr., B.S.E.E.

---

and Hynes, Brullo and I should have drafted the terms and conditions of the settlement agreement.

If that were the case, the agreement that I signed would not have looked anything like the one I signed on December 8, 2004, and the world knows that to be the truth. Therefore, they could have never removed me. I would have requested $5,000 in legal fees plus back-pay with interest, and when the agency did not pay me by the next pay period, I would have contacted the judge or Hynes about the money. I believe Friedman knew that he willfully manipulated the settlement agreement, as part of an agency conspiracy to remove me without due process, using the LCA document by bypassing the Collective Bargaining Agreement.

Why was I not allowed to be present during my MSBP settlement discussion? Just consider the fact that one of the elements in the LCA states that I forfeit my rights to defend myself--really? I think, if I had a jury trial, I could make a strong case for signing the LCA under duress, if I had to. However, I'm sure with all the facts on the front end, it should not get to this point, but I would like to see all parties held accountable before the law.

I hate to mention this dirty little fact if my argument proves to be correct and what I have revealed here is a true criminal act based on race and filing a false labor report with the state of New Jersey. I strongly feel that Friedman, the agency legal staff director who had unlimited power and control over every document in my personnel record (i.e. seventeen prior EEOC cases), along with the other agency conspirators, must all be held accountable for the disparate treatment over the years. I'm not sorry, but *"if the glove*

# Enemy Of The State

Disparate Treatment

James Coe Jr., B.S.E.E.

---

*doesn't fit, you must acquit"--Johnnie* Cochran

Before signing the LCA, I strongly questioned my legal counselor Kastner directly, several times, about the tone of the settlement agreement, only to be legally misrepresented by Kastner. I never willfully waived my grievance rights as stated in the last Chance Settlement Agreement. I also never willfully waived my MSPB Veterans Appeal Rights, nor did I willfully waive my EEOC Retaliation Rights. At the time, I was very uncomfortable, and I felt I had no options.

## THE ARBITRATION AWARD

Now, follow me here as I jump to page 4 of the text from the Union Arbitration Award Case No: 1A-00M-1A D05134186, Local No.: THO514, Robert Blum, Local Union Vice President (DNA#7).

## THE AWARD SUMMARY

"The Agency established that the Grievant violated the Last Chance Settlement Agreement. The Grievant stated that it was his decision not to testify. As such, the consistent and cumulative evidence and testimony offered by the Agency must be accepted as true and correct."

# Enemy Of The State

Disparate Treatment

James Coe Jr., B.S.E.E.

## THE DISPUTE ISSUE:

Did the Agency issue the Grievant a Notice of Proposed Removal for just cause in accordance with Article 16 of the National Agreement?

For the record, how is Arbitrator Joseph S. Cannavo, a one-time federal convicted felon, allowed to do Agency Arbitration Hearings? Cannavo affirmed my Notice of Removal based on the Last Chance Settlement Agreement, and, in his opinion, I did not speak in my defense during the hearing.

I need to make a few strong points here.

Firstly, the LCA was never signed by the agency and the union, which is a violation of the National Agreement. Should an experienced Federal Arbitrator like Joseph S. Cannavo not be aware of the National Agreement? Secondly, there clearly was no consistent grievance summary on record to match the event dates listed on the June 15, 2005 Decision.

Perhaps the true answer can be found in the text of the Last Chance Agreement itself. The text says, "I waive my grievance rights." But would I have honestly signed that document confirming that I waived my rights? As I stated before, I did not willfully waive them.

I should note here that unlike government court hearings with a court reporter, Arbitrations are not recorded, and the arbitrator is not a judge. That being said, the burden of proof is still on the Agency. The focus on the material facts

# Enemy Of The State

Disparate Treatment

James Coe Jr., B.S.E.E.

---

of April 1, 2005, when I was wrongfully placed on Emergency Placement In Off-Duty Status, did not change.

I find it very odd that a highly educated Disabled Veteran with a rare B.S. Degree in Electrical Engineering, who happens to be black, can be removed from government service without due process after working for seventeen years.

Apparently, if you're black, you can be removed anytime your bosses want you removed, without just cause or your right to a fair grievance free of disparate treatment under the National Agreement.

Cannavo used several quotes from the MSPB Last Chance Agreement (DNA#6).

One of the quotes reads: "Employees must follow instructions, and conduct themselves at work consistent with the rules and regulations; but that the agency can no longer suffer the Grievant's employment."

This agreement is not legal, because it changes my terms and conditions of employment without the written consent of the Union. In other words, it clearly violates the CBA. Why did the Arbitrator use an illegal LCA (DNA#6) to base his opinion on, given the fact it's not part of the grievance process? For the record, I do recall that the Emergency Placement In Off-Duty Status grievance was withdrawn in

# Enemy Of The State

Disparate Treatment

James Coe Jr., B.S.E.E.

Step 2 of the Grievance process by DuPree in a letter dated May 12, 2005. The dates in the Notice of Proposal are all before May 12, 2005.

What makes this story newsworthy is if you bypass the disparate treatment element, the Agency failed twice to make a prima facie case at the MSPB or show just cause at the New Jersey Appeal Tribunal. Add to the history that several high level government officials conspired to limit my employment rights and make false reports makes this a criminal case. I think if the U.S. Justice Department investigates under the Whistleblower Act, or whatever law they choose, there can only be no just cause. They are going to find all the recorded testimony from the Merit System Protection Board and New Jersey Labor Department consistently supports a no just chance finding!

In fact, Dave Friedman, Esq., the agency damage control mastermind, if not removed for misconduct over the years, is the only official with the authority to make me whole with back pay and other benefits. Until the war ends, I will be on the streets of America fighting back. This respectful veteran has earned the rights, the Freedom, and the Independence the government has wrongfully denied him. I am not going to allow the government or its agents to take away my Freedom without a fight to my death!

## THE U.S. JUSTICE DEPARTMENT

# Enemy Of The State

Disparate Treatment

James Coe Jr., B.S.E.E.

The smoking gun here is, if the U.S. Justice Department investigates the fact that under the National Agreement, no one other than the Union can waive the employee's legal rights, and since the Union did not sign the Last Chance Settlement per the National Agreement, it is legally unenforceable in any *"administrative process"* including Arbitration. Lastly, I should mention again, Senior Plant Manager Victor Pacheco signed both the LCA and the Letter of Decision, before this arbitrator. This fact alone clearly demonstrates a conflict of interest under the National Agreement.

# Enemy Of The State

Disparate Treatment

James Coe Jr., B.S.E.E.

# Enemy Of The State

Disparate Treatment

James Coe Jr., B.S.E.E.

## Chapter 5: The Workplace Matrix

### I'M UNDER GOVERNMENT ATTACK

I'm a firm believer that people tend to follow complex information better when it's in the form of a metaphor or an analogy. Therefore, the plan starting here is to pull back the curtains and share with you my work history before the (PPP) Prohibited Personnel Practice on April 1, 2005, which is a fancy term for what I did wrong (i.e. was accused of) that landed me in the unemployment line. I also must warn that the facts may be offensive, but the facts are still the facts. They are necessary to put my employment experience in real-life context. Stated another way, this will allow the reader to walk in my size twelve shoes.

First, let me state for the case record that I'm a member of several so called legally protected groups: the 1964 Equal Employment Opportunities Commission Act (EEOC), the Vietnam Era Veteran's Preference Act, the Age (40+) Discrimination Employment Act, and Race (Black) Employment factor. In addition, as a government employee, I'm also protected by a National Collective Bargaining Agreement, sometimes called the CBA.

---- This is the beginning of the story context before any adverse personnel action ----

If you recall, in chapter one, I mentioned several instances

# Enemy Of The State

Disparate Treatment

James Coe Jr., B.S.E.E.

in which I was ridiculed and discriminated against at the federal agency where I worked.

I worked in this very hostile workplace for seventeen years and three months where unchecked racial harassment was the norm, and from the beginning, I was blacklisted.

I was denied employment advancement at every opportunity.

The U.S. Postal Service was a hostile work environment that allowed New York Metro Senior Staff Legal manager David Freidman to operate above the law without accountability to any higher authority.

To put things into context, recall the times I mentioned in chapter one of being called a "nigger" multiple times, of finding a monkey doll with a noose around it's neck with my name tag on it, of finding my car keyed, of being likened to O.J. Simpson and other black men in the newspapers, etc. Most importantly, don't forget the time that I was kicked in the groin by a white co-worker (Frank Garonski) in front of other white co-workers.

As stated before, Frank's only punishment for physically assaulting me was a three-day suspension, due to my filing an EEOC report. As well, each instance of harassment was reported to SDO Brullo to no avail.

Over the course of my employment, I filed twelve EEOC reports. In most of these cases, David Friedman was in charge of damage control, and my complaints were swept under the rug.

# Enemy Of The State

Disparate Treatment

James Coe Jr., B.S.E.E.

---- This is the end of the story context before any adverse personnel action----

Now let's fast forward to the prohibited personnel policy, which the agency later used to remove me without just cause.

Given my educational background, I applied for twenty-one Technology Promotions during my seventeen years of Postal Service Employment, only to receive a collection of twenty-one "better luck next time" letters. I recently discovered from the now retired EEOC Manager that for seventeen years, my direct report manager (SDO Brullo) never processed my requests for promotion in a timely manner, which would always result in my disqualification, based on the promotion announcement closing dates.

Prior to my removal from the United States Postal Service, I was diagnosed with Prostate Cancer, which caused me to frequent the men's room. The final EEOC Complaint that I filed (EEOC No.:1A-089-0015-05) was where SDO Brullo, who later retaliated by firing me, continued harassing me by following me into the men's room. I can provide co-workers to confirm the men's room harassment, which, for the most part, occurred every time my supervisor witnessed me entering the men's room. In fact, SDO Brullo would follow me into the men's room and position himself next to me at the urinal. I felt helpless because of the retaliation fear factor. Also, note that generally all supervisors used pass-key protected restrooms in the manager's office located in a secure part of the building. It was not standard operating procedure for managers to use the employees' restroom. If

# Enemy Of The State

Disparate Treatment

James Coe Jr., B.S.E.E.

anything, the employees' restroom was considered off-limits to management, except in cases of an emergency.

Over time, I became very uncomfortable with the behavior of SDO Brullo, as would any normal employee under these working conditions. At some point, I elected to open an EEOC Complaint (No: 530-2006-00176X, Agency No: 1A-089-0015-05) based on what I believed to be Sexual Harassment. It turns out the EEOC Investigator ruled that there could never be Sexual Harassment between the same sexes, i.e. male on male. This is, of course, an absurd assumption on his part. At some point shortly after, SDO Brullo was cleared by an in-house EEOC Investigation. Within thirty days, SDO Brullo threatened to fire me in retaliation for my protected EEOC activity.

The facts are clear: my federal employment rights to engage in protected EEOC Activity were unlawfully violated by the United States Postal Service the day I was led from the building by the Edison Police Department at the direction of SDO Tony Brullo, MDO John Szpyhulsky, and Plant Mgr. Victor Pacheco, and later removed based on a Union Arbitration Hearing conducted by a convicted Federal Felon, Joseph S. Cannavo, Jr. (Supreme Court of Missouri Case, No. 79938)

Recently, there have been several co-workers to come forward to affirm that the Union was guilty of collusion, which violates my due process rights by failing to represent me in good faith under the Collective Bargaining Agreement before Hearing Arbitrator Cannavo.

Additionally, if you compare Karen Lewicki's employment

# Enemy Of The State

Disparate Treatment

James Coe Jr., B.S.E.E.

history (same department, removed ten times during her twenty year Postal Service career), and Brian Stankiewicz (never removed for a workplace assault on a black manager) one can only wonder if this was not, at the least, *"Disparate Treatment"* by the Union and Postal Service Management team, given the fact that both employees were Caucasian and were later returned to Service by the same management team that wrongfully removed me.

The Last Chance Agreement, the controlling document used in this labor dispute, upon review, will be shown to be not legal or enforceable under the law. Therefore, the removal per New Jersey Labor Department of Labor Appeal Tribunal was grossly illegal and must be instantly reversed.

Also, under the Collective Bargaining Agreement, a Vietnam Era Veteran is a member of a protected class and must, therefore, be paid in full after a suspension of fourteen days or more, if he or she has not been found guilty of a criminal act.

Be advised that alleged workplace insubordination does not rise to the level of a criminal act.

In addition, it should be noted in the context of the pre-personnel action story line, that SDO Brullo, a Caucasian Postal Service Manager, had a work history of two physical workplace assaults (fighting), in which race was a reported factor, involving two black male co-workers, George Graham and Nate Lawrence. Upon completion of in-house investigations, both black employees were returned to duty by both the Local Union Branch and Postal Service Plant

# Enemy Of The State

Disparate Treatment

James Coe Jr., B.S.E.E.

Manager Pacheco.

At the end of the day, as a Vietnam Era Veteran, when you consider the context history and the credibility factor of SDO Brullo, and the New Jersey Department of Labor Hearing Ruling: *"We Find No Evidence of Employment Misconduct"*, this case simply does not support the final decision under the law which resulted in the wrongful removal of a Disabled Veteran from the United States Postal Service after seventeen years of service.

Once again, America: CAN you afford to deny black veterans equal justice under the law?

If I could write an ending to this story, it would be this:

This wrongful personnel action must be instantly reversed, and the disabled veteran in this case, Mr. Coe, must be made whole. In addition, those who approved this injustice against Mr. Coe must be held accountable for willful misconduct in the workplace.

# Enemy Of The State

Disparate Treatment

James Coe Jr., B.S.E.E.

# Enemy Of The State

Disparate Treatment

James Coe Jr., B.S.E.E.

## Chapter 6: The DNA Fingerprints Matrix

DNA#1: USPS EQUAL EMPLOYMENT OPPORTUNITY COMMISSION CASE

Reveals the nature of [EEOC No: 530-2006-00176X] and [Agency Case No: 1A-089-0015-05] in-house EEOC Discrimination Complaint based on Race and Sexual Harassment in the workplace against SDO Brullo before he was allowed to remove Mr. Coe based on hearsay evidence in the Notice Of Proposed Removal (DNA#8).

DNA#2: USPS Emergency Placement In Off-Duty Status Letter

DNA#3: Mail-Handlers Union – Step 1: Grievance Summary

DNA#4: New Jersey Appeals Tribunal

DNA#5: Merit Systems Protection Board Case History

DNA#6: MSPB - Last Chance Settlement/Agreement

DNA#7: Arbitration Award

DNA#8: USPS Notice of Proposed Removal

# Enemy Of The State

Disparate Treatment

James Coe Jr., B.S.E.E.

DNA#9: USPS Letter of Final Decision

DNA#10: Mail-Handlers Union - Step 2: Grievance Designee

Employee Comments:

Race discrimination is the common factor throughout this adverse agency action. If I were a white employee, this would never see the light of print! Where was the so called act of insubordination?

I was given this letter on April 1, 2005. I was escorted out of the facility by the Edison Police after SDO Brullo made a 911 call stating I was making terrorist threats in a government building on April 1, 2005. It would turn out that I was never allowed in the Kilmer P&DC facility after April 1, 2005.

I was given a Notice of Removal (DNA#8) by the Agency based on false hearsay evidence not related to the April 1, 2005 agency action.

I strongly request the U.S. Attorney General use the full power of the U.S. Government to investigate and correct the agency misconduct which has violated both my Veteran's and U.S. Civil Rights under the law.

The facts are clear. Several agencies had failed in the protection of my rights.

The records will show that during the USPS Employee Grievance process, the U.S. Merit Systems Protection Board

# Enemy Of The State

Disparate Treatment

James Coe Jr., B.S.E.E.

process, and the Equal Employment Commission, my rights to due process under U.S. law were grossly violated. This is a federal crime!

I will appeal to the U.S Justice Department to protect and to defend my civil rights under the U.S. law.

The criminal misconduct here is that the agency committed several unlawful acts: (1) criminal conspiracy when agency management filed a false labor relations report with the New Jersey Department of Labor, (2) disregarding my protected class Vietnam Era Veteran's Employment Act rights, (3) disparate treatment under the Collective Bargaining Agreement - - my discipline issued *"removal"* was not progressive, (4) regarding EEOC retaliation protection for prior activity.

Under the law, the U.S. Postal Service has failed to show just cause or establish a Prima Facie case. First, during the state unemployment administrative process, and later, at the federal Merit System Protection Board administrative process, and finally, at the Collective Bargaining Agreement Arbitration process.

## HISTORY VS. RACE

At the end of the day my argument is that race was the only motive; history has shown if you keep applying the same facts, and you keep getting the same outcome... *"If the glove doesn't fit, you must acquit"* -Johnnie Cochran-

# Enemy Of The State

Disparate Treatment

James Coe Jr., B.S.E.E.

---

The fact that the agency withheld witness statements and critical documents from the Union per the Collective Bargaining Agreement for two years, only to have the Arbitrator, Joseph S. Cannavo Jr. in DNA#7, (a U.S. convicted felon), allow two year old evidence into testimony on October 10, 2007, violates the terms and Conditions of employment under the National Agreement grievance process.

The Agency's misconduct is clearly based on a foundation of hearsay evidence which could not survive a jury trial.

The Agency's criminal activity must be fully investigated by the U.S. Justice Department.

The major USPS/Agency players with knowledge to be investigated in full or in-part:

USPS' damage control legal mastermind, David Friedman, Esq. Friedman has total legal knowledge and process control from A-Z.

(DNA#7) - USPS/Arbitrator/Felon Joseph S. Cannavo Jr., disbarred by Missouri Bar in 1997. Reference: Missouri Supreme Court, No.79938 - Arbitration Case Decision

USPS/Plant Mgr. Victor Pacheco - Letter of Final Decision

USPS/MDO John Szpyhulsky - Notice of Proposed Removal

USPS/SDO Tony Brullo - Notice of Proposed Removal, Emergency Placement Off-Duty Status, New Jersey Labor Dept. Report

# Enemy Of The State

Disparate Treatment

James Coe Jr., B.S.E.E.

It's dangerous to be right when the government is wrong!

I was wrongfully denied multiple U.S. Civil Rights violations in multiple government venues using hearsay evidence fraud.

I was denied the opportunity to add unlawful retaliation to my EEOC complaint (1A-089-0015-05) (DNA#1), which would show SDO Brullo retaliated against me on April 1, 2005 when he issued an Emergency Placement Off-Duty Letter, DNA#2, and a Notice of Proposed Removal, DNA#8.

Anything less, at this point, is an unlawful criminal act. Remember the fact that I was unlawfully barred and locked out of the USPS building. Why?

I didn't have access to the Union, nor did they contact me.

This was unlawful. So, how does one protect his or her rights under this type of terrorism?

Per law, a Vietnam Era Veteran cannot be in a non-pay status for over fourteen days. After this point, the agency must pay him 100% salary until he has been convicted of a criminal act.

I shall reference SDO Brullo's Step 1: Grievance Summary as well as the New Jersey Appeal Tribunal Decision. In that decision, the appeal tribunal found no misconduct.

Mail-handler's National Agreement Article 16.10

# Enemy Of The State

Disparate Treatment

James Coe Jr., B.S.E.E.

---

"The record of a disciplinary action against an employee shall not be considered in any subsequent disciplinary action if there has been no disciplinary action initiated against the employee for a period of two years." This sounds like the verbiage used in the LCA, which the Union was denied from witnessing.

The Last Chance Settlement entered into on December 8, 2004 at the MSPB Docket# PH-0752-05-0067-I-1 and PH-0752-04-0579-I-1, were unlawful for three points: (1) disparate treatment, (2) union failed to witness and co-sign the LCA documents (3) the LCA changed my terms and conditions of employment, which violates Article I of Collective Bargaining Agreement.

The smoking gun here is the fact that my paid Attorney Mitchell Kastner, an experienced federal employment lawyer and a former Merit System Protection Board sitting Judge himself, should have reasonably known every detail listed here and more.
I think it's fair to say my attorney threw me under the bus at the MSPB Hearing on December 8, 2004.

In the paragraph above I tried to list most of the misconduct and disparage of treatment I suffered during the administrative process before the final decision was made on June 15, 2005 by Senior Plant Manager Victor Pacheco to wrongfully remove me from the Postal Service effective as of that date. In no case may a supervisor impose suspension or discharge upon an employee unless the proposed discipline action by the supervisor has first been reviewed and concurred, in a signed and dated writing, by the installation head or designee. How do you prove a

# Enemy Of The State

Disparate Treatment

James Coe Jr., B.S.E.E.

criminal conspiracy gone wild?

## CONSIDER THE MATH HERE TO PROVE A MISCONDUCT CONSPIRACY:

If two or more, in my case three managers and three attorneys, partner-up to deny my Vietnam Era Veteran's Rights this is criminal collusion. There is no other way to say it: race was the only factor.

In this case, Victor Pacheco concurred in writing (conspiracy-collusion) in Pacheco's "letter of Final Decision" per the National Agreement (DNA#9).

What I find criminal is how does a ten year agency senior plant manager not know the National Agreement labor relations administrative process from A to Z with regard to the grievance process?

I am 100% sure that I'm not the first employee Pacheco has removed from the agency. In fact, I can name one other employee.

At the end of the day, when it comes to race and you're a black, the National Agreement does not apply equally with regard to disparate treatment.

Keep in mind that I am a highly educated black employee. I, as a veteran, earned my B.S. in Electrical Engineering from one of the nation's top Universities, Temple University. This makes me a unique member of a professional group of

# Enemy Of The State

Disparate Treatment

James Coe Jr., B.S.E.E.

which only 1.7% of blacks earn a B.S. Electrical Engineering degree.

Despite this, I was denied employment advancement, every single promotion opportunity, over my seventeen year career at the USPS.

After connecting all the dots, I can see a clear racist pattern on the part of the management. The fact of the matter was that the management team of Pacheco, Szpyhulsky, and Brullo never approved my promotional applications in a timely manner. I am certain this was the strategy the agency used to deny me advancement.

Race based discrimination has not changed, and your Race does matter at the USPS. My unlawful removal proves it!

I'm a Vietnam Era Disabled Veteran who has served his country with honor. I have earned the right to force the agency to show just chance under the law. I pray, per the U.S. law, that the U.S. Justice Department corrects this criminal conspiracy misconduct.

In order to do this, they must start with the New Jersey Appeal Tribunal Docket #85,928.

Next, they must review the Step 1: Grievance Summary and then, the LCA and the Arbitration Award. The latter two are both illegal, but they do add some spice to the main event.

The Step 1: Grievance Summary is what I'm calling the "main event". The smoking gun in this story is the Step 1: Grievance Summary because, strangely enough, after you

# Enemy Of The State

Disparate Treatment

James Coe Jr., B.S.E.E.

---

read it a few times, the truth settles in at some point.

The legal question to date is how does a veteran of color find himself removed after seventeen years of government service for alleged misconduct without the government showing just cause?

I passionately find government misconduct (per the National Agreement under the disciplinary process), applying non-progressive and false disciplinary action, racial harassment, EEOC Retaliation, and disparage treatment all unforgivable criminal acts!

Can there be a bigger crime than government misconduct?

After all, what did my statement of "you followed me into the bathroom" have to do with the work? If the management staff has their own management restroom and lunchroom in the manager's office, explain why no other manager uses the employees' restroom? Why did SDO Brullo end up in the same restroom next to me over ten times before April 1, 2005?

I also feel I should mention something else in regards to April 1, 2005.

As I stated in a previous chapter, I was working the Low Cost Tray Sorter. It needs to be put into context here that normal post operating procedures is to always have a dispatch clerk working to dispatch the post-cons whenever the LCTS is operational. On April 1, 2005, all the post-cons were full and needed to be dispatched by the dispatch clerk on duty. I requested help to get them replaced by the

# Enemy Of The State

Disparate Treatment

James Coe Jr., B.S.E.E.

---

dispatch clerk, who should have been working the lanes. Under the rules of the National Agreement, a Mail-Handler craft employee cannot do work outside his union craft. During the insubordination event, both SDO Brullo and MDO Szpyhulsky failed to note this little detail, but it is consistent with my request for help, which SDO Brullo mentions in the Step 1: detail facts.

# Enemy Of The State

Disparate Treatment

James Coe Jr., B.S.E.E.

## Chapter 7: The Smoking Guns Matrix

If you like the title of this book, it's not why you think. Consider my definition of the magic bullet matrix, which is to apply a manipulation strategy during the labor dispute administrative process in order to determine the outcome. Now let's get started.

Imagine you're working in a high security government building and your supervisor (SDO Brullo) makes a 911 police call.

During the call, Brullo says "employee X" is making terrorist threats in the building.

What do you think the reaction of the police is going to be? Plus, this is now on the record, in some government computer, under your name. So, the police come. After some Q&A, the police informed me I was a victim of management abuse of power, and if I ever needed a witness concerning their police report, I just needed to make a request.

I shall respectfully withhold their names for now.

By the way, all police in blue are not all bad. I have made many friends on the job over the years. In fact, I had to make a sheath visit to the FBI, during which I discovered I had made the NSA's top 100 bad guys list. I feel very special but not honored to make the list.

# Enemy Of The State

Disparate Treatment

James Coe Jr., B.S.E.E.

At some point, I noticed my telephone calls were being tapped.

On April 1, 2005, I earned my first government promotion after twenty years. I was officially promoted by U.S. Homeland Security to the position of "Enemy of the State", pay grade zero, which means, that I would get zero government income going forward.

All I had to do now is fight back.

NSA now reads my e-mails and listens to my phone calls.
I even discovered and removed a key stroke logger from my laptop. I once did a search for Local Area Networks in my area. I was not surprised when I saw NSA in my network listing.

I feel like I am in a Die Hard movie.

In my world, even local traffic stops are very interesting now because, the local police cannot access my identity per NSA. In addition, the employees at the local Social Security Administration office need a supervisor level password clearance to access my Social Security records.

This is big brother watching your every move.

This is your government at work.

The fact that I'm a Veteran means zero at NSA intake point! At the end of the day, you're just another social security number on their watch list.

# Enemy Of The State

Disparate Treatment

James Coe Jr., B.S.E.E.

May God help me, if I run a red light.

When the government is wrong, there must be transparency which results in total legal liability. When the government commits gross misconduct against its citizens, the penalty must be massive, and the citizens must never suffer or be harmed in any way as a result of government misconduct.

The magic bullet here was when SDO Brullo and others pre-planned my notice of proposed removal, before April 1, 2005.

On April 1, 2005, (Tony Brullo), a federal government agency supervisor conspired with MDO Szphyhulsky to commit "fraud" by filing a false agency "Emergency Placement In Off-Duty Status" Report with the New Jersey Labor Department.

After a full investigation by the New Jersey Labor Department's "Appeal Tribunal", stated N.J.S.43:21-5(b), the claimant was not discharged for misconduct connected with the work. In addition, the New Jersey Labor Appeal Tribunal formally requested the federal agency reinstate me, a protected class disabled Vietnam Era Veteran, with full back pay and benefits.

The agency was fined $3000 for filing a false report.

What the government doesn't tell you could be dangerous for your quality of life!

# Enemy Of The State

Disparate Treatment

James Coe Jr., B.S.E.E.

## THE NSA TERROR WATCH LIST

Compliments of SDO Brullo's April 1, 2005 911 call, somewhere deep inside the United States government is a closely guarded list with my name on it.

Members of Congress never get to see this list, only the President and a secret team of advisors.

Once your name is on the terror watch list, it doesn't come off ... until you're dead.

## THERE ARE NO RIGHTS IF YOU CANNOT DEFEND THEM

I am not an attorney; however, to protect my rights, I'm forced to play one. I'm forced by the Merit Systems Protection Board and Homeland Security (NSA) to play a combo Labor Relations & Constitutional Civil Rights attorney in real life.

## YOU MUST KNOW YOUR LEGAL OPTIONS

The three Administrative Appeals Process jurisdictions of record:

The First is for veteran's rights protection, (MSPB) the

# Enemy Of The State

Disparate Treatment

James Coe Jr., B.S.E.E.

---

Merit System Protection Board.

The Second is the U.S. Appeals Court.

The Third is the U.S. Equal Employment Opportunity Commission Office of Federal Operations.

The U.S. Justice Department has the power and the authority to enforce any Federal or State Laws, especially in cases of 1964 Civil Rights Act or U.S. Constitutional violations.

*Note: The USPS must not be allowed to investigate EEOC complaints in-house.*

It's a serious red flag every year when the number of United States Postal Service Equal Employment Opportunity Commission discrimination complaints increases year-to-year in the Postal Service.

In my career alone, I was forced to file twelve complaints over a seventeen year span. The USPS operates in a culture of workplace racism.

Beware fellow American workers: your daily freedoms come at a very high price. If you don't fight to protect your freedoms, one by one, the government will take them away. In time, you will end up like me: homeless and poor, at the mercy of dead-end government welfare programs.

I am just asking ... do you want to end up like me?

# Enemy Of The State

Disparate Treatment

James Coe Jr., B.S.E.E.

Never let that happen. Fight back; support me!

During the adverse action administrative process, there were two errors: the first error by the Merit System Protection Board, which resulted in the LCA which the union never endorsed (DNA#6), and the second error was the National Agreement Arbitration Award (DNA#7), which affirmed the Last Chance Settlement, which as I stated before, the union failed to cosign, thus making the document unenforceable.

## THE THREE ADMINISTRATIVE APPEALS PROCESSES DOCUMENTS

* New Jersey Labor Appeal Tribunal

* Last Chance Settlement Agreement

* Union Arbitration Hearing

The New Jersey Appeal Tribunal Docket #: 85,928

The results of an independent state investigation (DNA#4) find under New Jersey Labor Department law, there was no misconduct by the claimant, in this opinion, Mr. Coe (me). They recommended I be reinstated with full benefits.

They also provided evidence of fraud on the part of the agency officials for filing a false labor report.

Finally, they fined the agency for filing a false report.

# Enemy Of The State

Disparate Treatment

James Coe Jr., B.S.E.E.

---

Merit System Protection Board DKT: PH-0752-04-0579-I-1 (DNA#5)

1. The Appellant claims the Board made gross errors when it recommended a Last Chance Settlement, which was illegal and unenforceable.

There were multiple points in the LCA which violated both the CBA rights and the Civil Rights of the appellant. No MSPB settlement can legally deny any appellant their rights to due process under the law. The appellant always has the right to appeal any adverse actions against an appellant for the life of the settlement. The appellant cannot be misled, using collusion, into waiving his right to appeal.

Looking back now, the agency, under the direction of damage control mastermind David Friedman, Esq., had a master plan, which was to allow thirty days to pass by. Then the agency's removal plan could never be appealed to MSPB, because the window of appeal would be forever closed. Any appeal filed after thirty days would be untimely under the MSPB appeal rules.

None of the parties can use LCA to gain an unfair advantage over the other party.

More specifically, no party can take away another party's constitutional right to defend themselves in the jurisdiction that has authority over the parties, if falsely harmed under the agreement.

# Enemy Of The State

Disparate Treatment

James Coe Jr., B.S.E.E.

---

The Collective Bargaining Agreement prohibits any employee from making any Settlement which changes the terms and conditions of the employee without the written consent of the union and the agency.

The fact that the Union failed to sign the LCA makes the agreement null and void.

What jurisdiction has authority over the settlement after thirty days?

The Union failed to sign it.

The MSPB window of enforcement is thirty days.

First off, it's only fitting that the Arbitrator, Joseph S. Cannavo, is a convicted federal felon. If you're out to commit misconduct you need to hire criminals with experience!

Where is Homeland Security when I need them?

DNA#1

I had an open EEOC Harassment complaint less than thirty days old against SDO Brullo before SDO Brullo signed a Notice of Proposed Removal. This is clearly EEOC retaliation misconduct. I think I made my point; where do I go for relief?

At the end of the day, it's dangerous to be right when the government is wrong!

# Enemy Of The State

Disparate Treatment

James Coe Jr., B.S.E.E.

Wish me luck!

# Enemy Of The State

Disparate Treatment

James Coe Jr., B.S.E.E.

# Enemy Of The State

Disparate Treatment

James Coe Jr., B.S.E.E.

About the author:

"I attended Temple University on the G.I. Bill after finishing my military tour of duty were I earned a Bachelor of Science. The discipline that I gained in the military, coupled with the University's commitment to veterans' re-entry into civilian life, enabled me to be successful in my studies and beyond.

For more information contact me below:

James Coe Jr.

P.O. Box 6992

Piscataway NJ 08854

www.ingramcontent.com/pod-product-compliance
Lightning Source LLC
Chambersburg PA
CBHW071804170526
45167CB00003B/1169